OF THE

PROPHETS

Other Books and Materials by Kris Vallotton

Developing a Supernatural Lifestyle: A Practical Guide to a Life of Signs, Wonders, and Miracles

Fashioned to Reign: Empowering Women to Fulfill Their Divine Destiny (book, workbook, leader's guide and video segments available individually, or as an all-inclusive curriculum kit)

God's Most Beautiful Creation (a six-part DVD or CD teaching series on women)

Heavy Rain: Renew the Church, Transform the World

Moral Revolution: The Naked Truth about Sexual Purity

Outrageous Courage: What God Can Do with Raw Obedience and Radical Faith (the Tracy Evans story; co-authored with Jason Vallotton)

School of the Prophets: Advanced Training for Prophetic Ministry (book, workbook, leader's guide and video segments available, or an all-inclusive curriculum kit)

Spirit Wars: Winning the Invisible Battle against Sin and the Enemy (book, workbook, leader's guide and video segments available, or an all-inclusive curriculum kit)

The Supernatural Power of Forgiveness: Discover How to Escape Your Prison of Pain and Unlock a Life of Freedom (co-authored with Jason Vallotton)

The Supernatural Ways of Royalty: Discovering Your Rights and Privileges of Being a Son or Daughter of God (co-authored with Bill Johnson)

Basic Training for the Supernatural Ways of Royalty (workbook)

Basic Training for the Prophetic Ministry (workbook)

School
OF THE
PROPHETS

Advanced Training for Prophetic Ministry

KRIS VALLOTTON

Chosen

a division of Baker Publishing Group

Minneapolis, Minnesota

Published by Chosen Books
11400 Hampshire Avenue South
Bloomington, Minnesota 55438
www.chosenbooks.com

Chosen Books is a division of
Baker Publishing Group, Grand Rapids, Michigan

Printed in the United States of America

ISBN 978-0-8007-9622-8

Cover design by Dan Pitts

15   16   17   18   19   20   21   7   6   5   4   3   2   1

I would like to thank Trish Konieczny
for her excellent work on this
curriculum project.

CONTENTS

LAUNCHING A
SCHOOL OF THE PROPHETS
GROUP

Once you have decided to launch a group study of *School of the Prophets*, you can approach it in a number of ways. Whatever approach you choose, I trust the end result will be the same—a better understanding of how to develop a strong and healthy prophetic community, along with how to engage in more effective prophetic ministry.

The *School of the Prophets Curriculum Kit* contains everything you need to make these end results a reality, with one exception. You and your group members will need that power from on high Jesus talked about when He told His disciples, "You will receive power when the Holy Spirit has come upon you; and you shall be My witnesses both in Jerusalem, and in all Judea and Samaria, and even to the remotest part of the earth" (Acts 1:8). To develop a thriving prophetic community and to lead those with the gift of prophecy or a call to the office of prophet or prophetess, you will need the presence of the Holy Spirit in attendance at your group meetings. Make sure to invite Him in and give Him room to work in you and through you as you lead your group through this *School of the Prophets* study.

Let's take a look at the different ways you could launch and lead a *School of the Prophets* study. As you choose an approach and formulate a plan, consider your situation, seek the Lord's direction, take stock of the resources you have available and ask Him for His creativity.

Church Life Group or Small Group Approach

Many churches offer life groups or small groups that meet regularly outside the church, usually in someone's home. Such a group provides an ideal setting in which to study *School of the Prophets*. Your church may already have such groups in place. If not, you may want to suggest forming them, at least temporarily, for the purpose of this study. Each group would meet for eight or nine sessions (usually once a week) specifically to focus on the material presented in *School of the Prophets*.

Each group that forms should include at least four or five people to facilitate discussion, with a maximum of ten or twelve people. Groups larger than a dozen make it difficult for everyone to give input and receive feedback effectively. Larger groups can divide into more numerous, smaller groups or move toward a church class approach (which I will discuss next). Here are the essentials for leading a group study:

- A consistent meeting place, either in the leader's home, another home or a space the church provides.

- Adequate technology in the form of a DVD player/TV/computer large enough and loud enough for all the group members to see and hear. (A small laptop playing at the far end of a room may make it difficult for a dozen people to get the most out of the teachings.)

- A committed leader/facilitator who is familiar with the material ahead of time and who is willing to follow the lead of the Holy Spirit as the group moves through the teachings. This could be an individual, or it could be a team, perhaps husband/wife hosts or two church leaders working together. The leader(s) will direct the sessions from beginning to end and perhaps call group members or send them online reminders about the meetings.

- A plan or schedule for the group meetings to keep them flowing through the various elements that will occupy the group's time together—fellowship, worship, prayer, a video teaching, discussion and ministry time. (Two sections ahead, in "Formatting Your Group Sessions," I provide a sample schedule that I think will work well for group meetings.)

Once you have these leadership essentials in place, you are ready to set a date for your first session and sign people up to take part in your group.

■ Church Class/Midweek Meeting/Sunday School Approach

In addition to weekend services, most churches offer some kind of church classes to disciple members and help them grow. These classes often cover a wide variety of topics that change from time to time, and meeting times may range from midweek services to Sunday school classes to some other agreed-upon time like a Saturday morning Bible study. Any of these models could lend itself to a study of *School of the Prophets*.

Since a large number of people are usually involved in such classes, the discussion element of a *School of the Prophets* study (or any other study) may become more of a challenge than it would be in a smaller group, but leaders can still encourage some dialogue. Also, because of time constraints, it may be necessary to extend the number of weeks to allow sufficient time for the class to work its way through the study. For example, a class could take two weeks to cover each session. One week could be devoted to watching a video segment for a particular session of the *School of the Prophets* study and talking about the principles I present in the video and in the book readings. The following week could be devoted to class discussion of the questions and life applications involved in that session.

Although small groups are an ideal approach to this study and are the model I had in mind as I put together this curriculum kit, you can certainly adapt a class approach as an effective model to get these principles across to a larger group already accustomed to meeting at a regular time. The ability to increase our understanding of prophetic ministry does not change based on the size of the group or the setting. If you will give the Holy Spirit room to work, you can effectively teach *School of the Prophets* in a variety of settings. Do not feel that the effects of this study will be limited if you need to adopt more of a classroom approach.

■ Church-wide Group Study Approach

In this approach, the pastor and senior leadership of a church decide to take the entire church through a study of *School of the Prophets* together. Weekend sermons would focus on the principles presented in the book and video segments (and some video clips might be shown in services). Sunday school/midweek classes/small groups would all focus on some aspect of the study, perhaps watching the video teachings together and discussing the questions and life applications.

The church-wide approach could be presented as *40 Days of Advanced Training for Prophetic Ministry* (reflecting the eight sessions of five daily studies each in the workbook). Each congregant could be encouraged to make the most of the church-wide focus by reading the *School of the Prophets* book, going through the workbook and participating in group sessions.

This approach is a great way to get everyone in a church body moving in the same direction, toward acknowledging the importance of both the gift of prophecy and of those called to the office (who are gifts themselves) within the Church. It is especially effective if a small group component is added to the overall church focus.

■ Individual Study Approach

As I said, I had group studies in mind when I designed this kit. Where there is no group study or church focus available to take part in, however, individuals can use the *School of the Prophets* book, workbook and video segments on their own to explore with me some ways to develop a healthy prophetic community and ministry in today's Church.

With the Holy Spirit as teacher and guide in an individual study of these materials, a person can learn from the Scriptures how prophets of the past played a different role from modern-day prophets and how the crossroads of the cross changed everything we knew about prophetic ministry. Again, the Holy Spirit's effectiveness is not limited to a certain size group or a certain setting. But if there is a group study to join, I do recommend that approach because of the fellowship, encouragement and discussion opportunities such a group can provide.

Preparing to Lead

While format should never replace flexibility when it comes to following the lead of the Holy Spirit, in a group setting the presence of the Lord is stewarded best in the midst of organization. Someone has to oversee the practical preparations for a group study, watch over the time schedule, facilitate the flow of the meeting and the ministry and pray for the group ahead of time. That someone will be you as the group leader or class facilitator. Let me give you some guidelines that will help you prepare to lead this study and minister to the participants.

Prepare with Prayer

I am sure it goes without saying that your first step in preparing to lead a *School of the Prophets* group is prayer. You have already prayed for the Lord's direction and determined that you are supposed to lead a group through this study. Continue to pray for increased insight on your part into the ability to develop and lead prophetic people and communities, and pray for a deeper understanding of the spiritual principles you will be covering as you lead the group. Spend some time with the Holy Spirit, asking Him to give you vision for what this study can accomplish in your life and the lives of the participants.

Session by session, pray for your group or class meetings ahead of time, and pray for the individuals who will attend. Be ready and willing to entertain questions, and be patient and persistent as you guide the group through these materials. For many, the idea of the prophetic *office* being different from the *gift* of prophecy will become clear to them for the first time. Beyond that, the thought of being proactive in developing healthy prophetic communities may be a new concept altogether. There is much to learn, and the Lord is about to do a marvelous work in the life of each person in your group as you walk through these sessions together.

Prepare with Study

Prepare to lead your *School of the Prophets* group by studying the material ahead of time yourself. Your first exposure to the principles contained in *School of the Prophets* should not take place in the middle of leading your group. By the time you meet for a session, you should have already read the assigned Scripture and book readings, watched the video segment, tackled the "Questions to Consider" yourself and made some life application in your daily walk.

In fact, I think it is a wise idea to work through the entire curriculum in this kit before taking on a leadership role, so that you are familiar with what is coming in each of the sessions. That will better prepare you to answer questions that may arise or direct the group to put a certain topic on hold until you reach the particular session that covers it. You will gain confidence and assurance to lead when you study ahead of time so that you will know where you are going with the group and how you will get there.

You do not need to be a brilliant academic scholar or hermeneutical expert to understand the material I present in *School of the Prophets*. While I was extremely careful with the scriptural scholarship required to put these truths on the printed page, they are truths understood more with the spirit than with the mind. Nonetheless, a little diligent scholarship can go a long way toward increasing the net spiritual effect of a study like this. As Jesus told us in Luke 6:39–40, "A blind man cannot guide a blind man, can he? Will they not both fall into a pit? A pupil is not above his teacher; but everyone, after he has been fully trained, will be like his teacher." If you will be diligent in your study to search out the truths contained in *School of the Prophets*, your group participants will see your familiarity with the material and the skill with which you handle it, and it will motivate them to be like you.

Prepare on a Practical Level

You have probably heard the saying that some Christians are so heavenly minded that they are no earthly good. It is true that you cannot wage war or take much territory for the Kingdom of God if you are so focused on heaven that you cannot walk out your faith powerfully while you are here on earth.

In other words, in addition to your preparation time in prayer and study, you need to prepare to lead on a practical level. If you will attend to the practical details, things will go much more smoothly in your group.

After you know which approach you are using, determine a meeting location that has sufficient space for your group and appropriate audiovisual equipment to play the video segments. The more comfortable you can make the setting, the more people will look forward to the meetings, without being distracted by issues like not enough seating or inadequate, uncooperative equipment. When you take care of the practical things ahead of time, you minimize distractions and give yourself credibility as a leader.

Once the place is all ready, set a schedule for your meetings. Pick a time period when your church calendar is not already filled with special events that will require large amounts of people's time. They will be more apt to commit to your group when they are not overcommitted in other areas. Check with other church leadership and the pastor(s) to make sure your proposed study does not conflict with anything major on the agenda, and then set a starting date. You should plan to follow the eight-session curriculum (or nine) consistently and consecutively to make the best use of your group's time together.

Once you establish a time period for your study, pick a day of the week and a time to meet (unless those are already determined in a church class or the like). It can be hard to accommodate everyone's work and home life schedules, but choose a day and time that will work best for the majority. Perhaps you can consider offering an alternate study at a future date for those unable to attend your current group.

Decide ahead of time about other practical matters such as whether your group will include refreshments or will make provision for childcare. Again, planning ahead in these areas can eliminate a host of distractions once your group begins. (I talk more about the specifics of planning your group time together in the section just ahead.)

Prepare to Get the Word Out

For a church-connected group study to succeed, church leadership must endorse it. Make sure your pastor and church leaders are aware of your proposed *School of the Prophets* study and are behind it. They can position themselves to help you with the launch by getting the word out.

Use multiple means, if possible, to let people at your church know a study group is forming and that they are invited to participate. See if an announcement can be made from the pulpit. Advertise the group on your church's website. Post a sign-up sheet and print flyers. Send out emails and post the event on your church's social media outlets. Make personal phone calls to individuals you sense should be involved in your group.

Prepare Potential Co-leaders or Assistants

Often, there will be people right in your group who are good candidates for co-leaders or assistants, and you may need them. Once you have a list of participant names, prayerfully consider whether there is someone on the list who is spiritually solid and mature, who could back you up during group ministry time or take your place leading the group in the event that you must miss a session.

Also think about names on the list who could assist with the practical side of things. Is there someone who enjoys working in the kitchen? Could that person oversee refreshments session to session or circulate a sign-up sheet so that you would not have to? Is there someone who enjoys children? Would that person be willing to plan activities for the group's children or make sure to enlist teens or other helpers to come in and do childcare for the couple hours that you meet? Is there someone on the list who enjoys showing hospitality? Might that person open his or her home to the group meetings and take care of the physical environment for you so that you can attend to the spiritual atmosphere?

You do not need to do everything yourself to lead a successful group. In fact, it might be better if you did not! Let the participants invest in the group by contributing to its welfare. There may be some who simply want to come, listen and learn, and go home, but others will be more than willing to help out if asked. They may even offer before you ask. Take them up on it!

Prepare Your Participants

As participants sign up for your group, let them know what they are getting into, so to speak. It might be a good idea to print out an information sheet that participants can take home as soon as they sign up. Listed on that sheet should be the time, place and dates of your sessions, along with the materials everyone involved in the group will need. Participants should each have a copy of *School of the Prophets* and the *School of the Prophets Workbook*. They will not need the leader's guide or the video segments/DVDs unless they plan to lead a group in the future. You, however, will need both to lead the group. You can purchase all the necessary materials together in one place in the *School of the Prophets Curriculum Kit*.

If your church has a bookstore, inquire about whether it can stock the *School of the Prophets* materials during the course of your group study (and beyond). You could also make the materials available for purchase at your sign-up table, or at least have copies on hand for participants to look at so they can find and order the book and workbook online. If you are able, it might also be good to have a few extra copies of both the book and workbook available for purchase at your first meeting, in case any latecomers join in and still need the materials. Your group will get off to a good start if you let everyone know how to obtain the *School of the Prophets* book and workbook quickly and easily so that they can get started with the study.

As they sign up, also let the participants know that *before* the group starts, they should work through Session 1 in the workbook, which includes readings from the book and from Scripture. That way, everyone will be on the same page and you can jump right in at that first meeting. The participants would then continue to work through one session per meeting, studying the material *prior* to each meeting. You could even consider including a syllabus on the information sheet that you hand out so that everyone can easily stay on schedule.

FORMATTING YOUR GROUP SESSIONS

As I said in the preparation section, format should not replace flexibility. It should, however, provide a foundation from which ministry can flow. If you have a dozen people in your *School of the Prophets* group and no format planned for your meetings, you will be pulled in a dozen different directions. As the group leader, it is your responsibility to come with a plan in hand, ready to direct the group. You may be led to follow the plan to the letter in all your meetings, or in some sessions the Holy Spirit may lead you in another direction. Either of those is fine, as long as you are prepared to start with a plan.

Several different elements can make up a group study. Some are necessary to this *School of the Prophets* study, while others are optional. The necessary elements are an introduction and opening prayer, time to watch the video segment, group discussion in which you talk about the video guide and the discussion questions, a "Life Application" review and group announcements about what to do to prepare for the next meeting. The optional elements are a time of worship, a fellowship/refreshments time and a group ministry time.

Pray and think through these elements, and then format a meeting schedule that incorporates the ones you will include. What follows is a sample schedule for an evening meeting that includes a few optional elements, along with the necessary ones. You can add or subtract from this sample schedule, adjusting it as needed to fit your group.

Sample Schedule: *School of the Prophets* Group Evening Meeting

- 6:15 Leader(s) arrive at meeting place (a home or other location) to connect with hosts/co-leaders/assistants. Make sure as leadership that you arrive on time. If you run late or come unprepared, your group members will sense the stress when they arrive. Frazzled, last-minute preparations put everyone on edge and prohibit a sense of peace and readiness. You will set an atmosphere for powerful ministry right from the start by being on time and coming well prepared for the evening.

- 6:15–6:30 Test all AV equipment for video viewing and/or worship to make sure everything is functioning properly. Have a backup plan in case of any malfunctions. Check on refreshments and childcare arrangements, if applicable. Review the evening's schedule with any assistants.

- 6:30–6:40 Pray together for the evening ahead. Possible prayer directives: for the Holy Spirit to move and minister freely; for the teaching to connect with and bring truth to all who hear it; for sensitivity to the Lord's direction in the leader(s); for conversation and discussion that edifies; for transparency and a close bond among group members; for life application of the lessons learned; for testimonies of the power of God at work through this study.

- 6:40–7:10 Do a final check to make sure you and your location are ready for the evening. Welcome group members as they arrive. Direct them to refreshments if those are provided, and make sure everyone has a comfortable spot. This is a good time to encourage fellowship among group members.

- 7:10–7:20 Gather everyone together. Have them bring their books and workbooks and prepare to get started. Welcome the group and briefly review with them which session and topics the meeting will cover. Pray for the evening aloud, or ask a group member to do so.

- 7:20–7:30 Worship time. Have someone lead a couple worship songs as you welcome the presence of the Lord at your meeting.

- 7:30–7:50 View the video segment applicable to the session you are covering. Suggest that group members fill in the video guide in their workbook as they watch.

- 7:50–8:20 Discussion time. Briefly comment on the video segment and give the answers to the video guide, then cover the session discussion questions contained in this leader's guide. Read the session questions aloud one by one (since the participant workbooks do not contain them), and ask group members for their comments. If time allows, also ask participants if there was anything in the session or the book itself that leapt out at them. Were there any ideas they struggled with? Anything that brought new understanding of a Scripture they had previously misunderstood? Engage in dialogue as a group to process this session's principles together.

- 8:20–8:30 Go over the "Life Application" section from the workbook and allow for a couple testimonies of what group members did as application and what resulted from their efforts. This important part of the *School of the Prophets* study brings the lessons home and helps group members apply them to daily life.

- 8:30 Bring the meeting to a close by reviewing which workbook session group members should work through in preparation for the next meeting. Offer a closing prayer and an opportunity for ministry to take place, if time allows. You could invite group members who want prayer to stay, and dismiss the rest.

CHECKLIST FOR LEADERS

■ One or Two Months Ahead

___ Have you determined the approach that is best suited for you to use for your *School of the Prophets* study? (If not, see the section titled "Launching a *School of the Prophets* Group.")

___ Have you determined a start and end date for your session meetings and checked your church calendar for possible conflicts? Have you picked a day and time that will allow for the most participation?

___ Have you secured a meeting location that will accommodate your projected group size and that has proper AV equipment?

___ Have you begun to advertise the *School of the Prophets* group study through your church, available social media and the like? Do you have a sign-up sheet ready?

___ Have you determined how and where to purchase materials and ordered your *School of the Prophets Curriculum Kit*? Do you have purchasing information ready for participants, who will need to buy or order their *School of the Prophets* book and *School of the Prophets Workbook* ahead of time?

___ Have you put together an information sheet to hand out to people who sign up for your group? It should list the meeting dates, time and location, as well as the materials group members will need and where they can get them.

■ Two to Four Weeks Ahead

___ Do you have your *School of the Prophets Curriculum Kit* in hand? Are you going through the material to familiarize yourself with it prior to leading the group study?

___ Have you read over the sample meeting schedule in the previous section, "Formatting Your Group Sessions," and adjusted it to fit the group you will lead?

___ If your meeting schedule will include elements such as worship or fellowship with refreshments, have you considered finding an assistant to help you oversee those areas?

___ Have you considered enlisting a co-leader, a spiritually mature believer who can help you in each session during ministry/prayer time and possibly lead a group meeting in the event of your absence?

One Week Ahead

___ Have you contacted those who signed up for your group to make sure they remember the starting date/time and are ready to begin?

___ Have you asked your participants if they have purchased the *School of the Prophets* book and workbook? Have you reminded them to go through Session 1 in preparation for your group's first meeting?

___ Have you double-checked all your AV equipment to make sure everything is in working order? Do you have a backup plan in place in case anything malfunctions?

One or Two Days Ahead

___ Have you reviewed Session 1 in the leader's guide, book and workbook so you are ready to handle questions and comments from the group? (It would be wise to review each session a day or two prior to your meetings.)

___ Have you contacted any assistants who are overseeing worship/refreshments/childcare to make sure they have everything in place?

___ Have you gathered your materials together so you are ready to walk out the door on time on the first meeting day?

First Meeting Day

___ Have you allowed yourself sufficient time to arrive at your meeting location early?

___ Have you looked over your meeting schedule again so you have the order of events in mind? (Keep in mind that the flow of ministry is facilitated by organization.)

___ Have you put on the full armor of God today? Then you are ready to go forth in power to minister through this study to those who prophetically minister to others. You will help both those who operate in the gift of prophecy and those who are called to the office to realize their full potential, purpose and power in Christ.

SESSION 1 GUIDE

Discovering Your Divine Call

In the following pages, I provide you with a step-by-step guide for each session to help you facilitate your group meetings. You can follow this guide, just as it is written, to take your group from start to finish as you go through the curriculum. If the Holy Spirit directs you to spend more time on one element and less on another, however, or to rearrange the elements in a certain meeting, by all means follow His lead! But again, planning a format for your meetings ahead of time gives you a solid foundation from which ministry can flow. These session guides provide you with that foundation.

This Session 1 guide gives more detailed instructions than the other session guides that follow because it sets the tone for the rest of your meetings. You can refer back to it from session to session, as needed, to refresh your memory about how to navigate through the different elements of your group time together efficiently. But each session guide repeats the basic elements and time allotments for you.

In each of these session guides, I provide the answers to the fill-in-the-blank video guide that participants will fill out in their workbooks as they watch the video segment. I also provide session discussion questions that I hope will encourage lively group dialogue. While the session discussion questions are not included in the participant workbooks, they are based both on the video segment and on the workbook's daily "Questions to Consider," which participants have already answered in preparation for your meeting.

In brief, Session 1 covers material from the Introduction and chapter 1 of *School of the Prophets*, along with the Session 1 pages from the participant workbook. In this session, I talk about the different streams of the prophetic, which can give rise to some prophetic white water we must navigate when those streams meet. I also talk about how pastoring prophetic people can be like herding cats, but how developing a healthy prophetic community is worth the effort. There is also a process in our personal development as prophets or prophetesses, and it is a process we cannot bypass. We need to let God establish us in our office by grace, because self-promotion without having both the favor of God and the favor of man can result in all kinds of personal and ministry issues. So can premature promotion that may come from "eager beaver" leadership. The timing of God is vital in walking out our prophetic call.

Leadership Prayer Focus (before the meeting): Ask the Lord to give your participants an awareness of how important walking in the timing of God is when it comes to prophetic ministry. Pray that they will have a clear understanding of the dangers of self-promotion and premature promotion, and that they will avoid both these scenarios and instead wait to be established in ministry by the grace of God.

Welcome and Fellowship Time (20–30 minutes): You should be ready 20 minutes before your meeting begins to start welcoming participants. Try to connect with each person as he or she enters the meeting place. Greet people, introduce them to others whom they may not know and direct them to enjoy some fellowship (and refreshments if applicable) until the group begins. Connectedness is important, and it starts with you as the leader. Many people attend small groups or church classes to learn and grow, but they miss out on making connections with other believers. You can help facilitate those connections by being available at the beginning of each session to greet participants as they arrive and introduce them to each other.

This would also be a good time to check with participants as they come in about whether they have the *School of the Prophets* book and workbook. Ideally, they will have purchased their materials and worked through Session 1 before this first meeting. That may not be the case for late sign-ups or some others, though. Try to have a few copies of both the book and the workbook available for purchase at your meetings so that everyone can follow along as you go through the materials.

Gather and Begin (10 minutes): Gather everyone together into the actual meeting area, inviting them to bring along their books, workbooks and something to write with. This first session (and any other sessions where there are newcomers), introduce yourself and outline the purpose of the group—to study *School of the Prophets* together and learn about developing a healthy prophetic community, along with gaining an understanding of the office of the prophet and prophetess in the Church today.

As an icebreaker, allow participants to briefly give their names and perhaps one interesting fact about themselves. (You can decide whether to do this only at the first meeting, or at every meeting.) Then discuss the meeting schedule with your group and briefly overview what your group sessions will look like. Make sure to mention that you will cover one session per meeting in the group, and that participants should read the materials and do the workbook pages for that session *prior* to the meetings.

Also take a few minutes at this first meeting to briefly orient participants to the book and workbook. (You can do this privately with newcomers at future sessions.) If you gave clear instruction about how to use the materials when people signed up to attend, most of them will have worked through Session 1 already and will be familiar with the curriculum. Mention, however, that as they work through the curriculum in preparation for each group meeting, the study involved will require a time commitment of 15–20 minutes per day (five days of readings and accompanying workbook pages per session). Encourage everyone to fully engage with the curriculum since they will get out of it as much as they put into it. The purpose for the daily assignments is not to add busywork to already busy schedules, but to cultivate a habit of Bible study and daily time in the presence of God as participants seek to understand more about prophetic ministry. Assure them that the results will be more than worth their time and effort!

If you are including an optional ninth session at which you plan to engage in some sort of social activity or have a meal together, you may want to mention that added session now so that everyone will realize that the curriculum materials will run for the first eight sessions, with the final ninth session being dedicated to wrap-up and fellowship.

Opening Prayer, Worship (10 minutes): Each session, pray for the meeting aloud, specifically addressing the topic you will be covering in your time together. Or you can ask a group member to pray aloud.

If your group includes a worship element, this time early in the meeting is a good place for worship since it stirs a hunger in people for God's presence and prepares their hearts to hear what the Holy Spirit has to teach them. If you or another group member can lead a few worship songs on an instrument or with your voice, that is wonderful. You can also worship with a CD or DVD, but make sure you have tested it and set it to the songs you have chosen ahead of time so that your transition into worship goes smoothly. (Technical difficulties can be a huge distraction to the flow of worship.) Or your group can sing a couple songs a cappella. The method of worship is not as important as the goal, which is to refresh believers in God's presence and draw them close to Him and to each other as your group meeting begins.

After worship opens the door, the atmosphere is typically charged with God's presence. It is not unusual for people to receive words of knowledge, wisdom or prophetic words in that atmosphere, or to experience other manifestations of the Holy Spirit. A group study such as this one is a great place in which people can "practice" these gifts and minister to each other. A word of caution, though: As group leader, it is up to you to steward your participants' time well. That means monitoring your group for distractions or disorder. Watch for people who might want to take charge of prayer or worship time inappropriately and distract from the order of the evening.

Once you sense that the Holy Spirit is ready for the group to move on, interject that those who wish to do so can come back to more prayer time at the end of the meeting, but that for now, you need to move on with the meeting schedule as planned.

Also watch for people who might seek to monopolize the group's time with their problems or who have issues requiring more specialized counsel than your group setting allows. Gently direct them to put their comments on hold and talk to you after the group study part of the meeting is concluded. Emphasize that it is important for the group as a whole to move through the materials as scheduled so that everyone present can get the most from the curriculum, but that you will come back to their concerns at a later point. At the end of the meeting, after the group has been dismissed, you can minister to such people in prayer or direct them to an appropriate counselor in the church who can help them further.

Video Teaching (20–30 minutes): At this point, transition into teaching time by having the group watch the video segment that goes along with Session 1. In it, I will touch on some topics the book has already covered, and I will also present some new insights into the material. Participants should have workbooks and pens in hand so they can fill in the video guide in the workbook as they watch and listen. In each video segment, I will give them all the information they need to fill in the blanks on the accompanying workbook page. Again, make sure to test and set up all AV equipment *prior* to your meetings so that when you push *PLAY*, the video plays without a hitch. Preparation is key when it comes to AV.

Here are the answers for the Session 1 video guide. Take a minute to review these answers with your group after the video so they can fill in any blanks they missed.

1. You shouldn't be <u>shocked</u> when you're praying and <u>Jesus</u> shows up.
2. It's not good to <u>argue</u> with the Lord; you can learn that from reading the <u>Bible</u>.
3. If you will spend your <u>life</u> bringing out the <u>best</u> in people, you will always have a <u>ministry</u>.
4. "He who <u>receives</u> a prophet in the name of a prophet shall receive a prophet's <u>reward</u>" (Matthew 10:41).
5. If God calls you, when it's time for Him to <u>anoint</u> you for that position, He will create some kind of <u>sign</u>, some kind of <u>wonder</u>, some kind of place—something that says to the rest of the people, "This person is called for this time to this people for this ministry."
6. When you are anointed, God will create a <u>pathway</u> from the <u>promise</u> to the <u>palace.</u>

Discussion/Dialogue Time (30–40 minutes): Now it is time to get your group members dialoguing about the things they are learning in this session.

Open up the dialogue with the following discussion questions. Some questions are new, from the fresh ideas I presented in the video segment. Others may revisit some of the questions I asked in the daily workbook pages for this session, so that participants have a chance to talk over their workbook answers and gain insight from each other. If there are Scriptures connected to a particular question, encourage participation by asking a group member to read the Scripture aloud. Then read the discussion question to the group and ask for input. Given the topics we cover in this *School of the Prophets* study, I do not think it will take long before you have a lively discussion going in every session meeting.

Session 1 Discussion Questions

1. When the Lord told Kris in his open vision in the bathtub, "History will tell us if you believe Me," what was He telling Kris about the role Kris had to play in fulfilling his destiny? What happens when we do not believe what the Lord is telling us because it seems so inconceivable? What happens when we do believe?

2. When Bill Johnson first introduced Kris to Bethel Church as a prophet, Kris said he felt as though he had been invited up into an office he had been called to but had never walked in. Walking in your calling does not usually happen immediately. As Kris put it in today's video, there is a pathway from the promise to the palace. What are some ways you can know the time is right to start walking in your call?

3. Kris commented in today's video that when he was introduced as a prophet to the church, people's levels of expectation changed. They were almost afraid of even sitting near him, thinking that he would know everything about their lives. As a prophet or prophetess, have you experienced that kind of reaction in people? How do you handle it?

4. In the closing prayer of today's video, Kris prayed that prophets and prophetesses would rise up and that "their words would become worlds." What do you think that statement means?

Life Application Check (10 minutes): Many participants leave a group study feeling that the teaching was insightful, the discussion lively and the meeting a success. But they also leave feeling that one important question went unanswered: "What do I do *next* to apply the principles I learned to my life and my spiritual walk?" To prevent that, I have included a "Life Application" section in every session of the participant workbook. Each application directs the participants to *do something* in response to what they learned through their study of the principles in that particular session. During your group meeting, it would be beneficial to spend a few minutes going over the "Life Application" section. Read the application aloud from the workbook and allow time for a couple testimonies of what group members did in response and what good things resulted from their efforts to apply this session to their lives.

If some participants have not done the application, urge them to go back and try it as soon as possible in the coming week. This is an important part of any study. It really brings the lessons home and helps people apply what they are learning to daily life. There would be little point in studying *School of the Prophets* at all if it had a net effect of zero on your life or ministry!

Closing Prayer/Ministry (time will vary): Make any announcements your group will need to be aware of before the next meeting. Make sure to include a mention of which workbook session your participants should work through in preparation for next time. (In this case, they should work through Session 2 in preparation for the next meeting.) Encourage everyone again to participate fully in the study by doing the five daily workbook sections and the readings that go along with those, so that they get the most out of the material. Then offer a closing prayer to wrap up your meeting, or ask someone in the group to do so, and dismiss the group members to return home.

Usually by the time you move through your meeting schedule and get to the closing prayer, some people will need to leave. If there are those present who desire prayer for anything specific, however, or who desire practice in prophetic ministry, you could invite them to stay, if time allows.

If the members of your group are not pressed for time by work schedules or family responsibilities, think about making this ministry time a regular element at the close of your meetings. Check ahead about whether your meeting place would allow for the group to stay a little longer, and then invite those who wish to stay to take part in prayer and in practicing prophetic ministry together after your meetings. This will give the Holy Spirit room to move in people's lives in response to the lessons they have learned. It is also a good way to take the life application practice even further, and it can provide a powerful conclusion to your meetings.

SESSION 2 GUIDE
New versus Old Testament Prophets

In brief, Session 2 covers material from chapter 2 of *School of the Prophets*, along with the Session 2 pages from the participant workbook. In this session, I cover the completely different roles of prophets in the New and Old Testaments. Why shouldn't the prophets and prophetesses of today pronounce judgment and call down fire on sinners, as in the days of old? Because at the crossroads of spiritual history, Jesus ushered in a New Covenant based on a ministry of reconciliation. In this session, we will take a close look at how prophetic ministry has changed completely this side of the cross because of what happened on the cross. Rather than being "Prophets of Doom," we now are called to be the salt of the earth, standing in the gap and preserving the world. The old contract of the Law has been made obsolete, and a violent grace has replaced it. God has made a way to both satisfy justice through the blood of the spotless Lamb and extend mercy to those who do not deserve it (us included), not counting their trespasses against them.

Leadership Prayer Focus (before the meeting): Ask the Lord to give your participants a burning heart for the ministry of reconciliation rather than a burning desire for judgment to fall. Pray that they would realize their role as the salt of the earth, not voices of doom and gloom. Ask the Holy Spirit to give each participant a new moment of decision at the crossroads of history, the cross, so that he or she can go in a new direction of prophetic ministry if some course correction is needed.

Welcome and Fellowship Time (20–30 minutes): Be ready 20 minutes before your meeting to start welcoming participants. Connect with each person as he or she arrives. Direct people to enjoy some fellowship (and refreshments if applicable) until the group begins. Check with any new participants about whether they have a *School of the Prophets* book and workbook, and help them get hold of the materials if needed. Ideally, participants will have worked through Session 2 by now, which is the material you will cover in this meeting.

Gather and Begin (10 minutes): Gather everyone together, along with their books, workbooks and something to write with. Introduce yourself and briefly outline the purpose of the group—to study *School of the Prophets* together and learn about developing a healthy prophetic community, along with gaining an understanding of the office of the prophet and prophetess in the Church today.

If you wish, allow participants to again give their names and perhaps one interesting fact about themselves, as they did at the first meeting. Briefly overview what the coming sessions will look like, and mention again that you will cover one workbook session per meeting and that participants should read the materials and do the workbook pages for that session *prior* to the meetings.

This might be a good time to ask your group members how their daily study time in preparation for the meetings has gone for these first two sessions. Encourage them to continue fully engaging with the curriculum to get the most out of this study. Also, if you are including an optional ninth session, remind the group again about that final meeting being dedicated to wrap-up and fellowship.

Opening Prayer, Worship (10 minutes): Pray for the meeting aloud, or ask a group member to do so. If your group includes worship, enter into that now to prepare your hearts to receive whatever the Holy Spirit has for you in this meeting. Remember as group leader to put in place ahead of time your method for worship and double-check AV equipment so that it functions properly. Be alert in this time of worship since people may receive words of knowledge, wisdom or prophetic words.

It is easy to get lost in worship, so remember that it is up to you to steward your participants' time well and monitor the group for distractions. Once you sense that the Holy Spirit is ready for you to move on into the study portion of your meeting, help the group make that transition. Gently direct those who might monopolize the group's time with personal problems or issues to put their comments on hold and talk to you after the group meeting is concluded. At that time, you can minister to them on a deeper level or direct them to an appropriate counselor in the church who can help them further.

Video Teaching (20–30 minutes): At this point, transition into teaching time by having the group watch the video segment that goes along with Session 2. Participants should have workbooks and pens in hand so they can fill in the video guide in the workbook as they watch and listen. The video segment will give them all the information they need to fill in the blanks, and you will review the answers with them after the video. Again, make sure to test all AV equipment *prior* to your meeting so that when you push *PLAY*, the video plays!

Here are the answers for the Session 2 video guide. Review these answers with your group after the video so they can fill in any blanks they missed.

1. The <u>root cause</u> of abortion and the root cause of almost every social dysfunction is the <u>lack</u> of understanding of the <u>love</u> of God.

2. In Matthew 5:44–45, Jesus said, "But I say to you, love your <u>enemies</u> and pray for those who persecute you, so that you may be <u>sons</u> of your Father who is in heaven; for He causes His sun to rise on the evil and the good, and sends rain on the righteous and the unrighteous." In the Old Covenant, it didn't rain on the <u>unrighteous</u>.

3. God knows the <u>hearts</u> of people, and we <u>don't</u>.

4. Your love for God in the <u>Old Covenant</u> was demonstrated by how much you <u>hated</u> people who hated God. Jesus lived in the Old Covenant but was <u>ushering</u> in the New one.

5. In a covenant <u>shift</u>, Jesus begins to talk to us about a new way to see the <u>world</u> . . . God is extending mercy to people who don't <u>deserve</u> it.

6. I didn't get into the Kingdom through my <u>works</u>; I got in through <u>His</u>.

7. It is true that the world deserves to be <u>judged</u>, but God doesn't <u>deal</u> with us through what we deserve, but through what <u>Jesus</u> deserves— and Jesus died for the sins of the world.

8. We live on the <u>mercy</u> side of the <u>cross</u>.

9. How did God <u>reconcile</u> the world? He didn't count their <u>trespasses</u> against them.

10. The main <u>ministry</u> of an Old Testament prophet was to <u>enact judgment</u> for sin.

11. You can't do it (keep the Law). That's the whole point of the Old Testament—it's a <u>tutor</u> that leads us to a <u>Savior</u>.

12. The <u>role</u> of the New Testament prophet has little to do with the <u>role</u> of the Old Testament prophet, especially as it pertains to <u>judgment</u>.

Discussion/Dialogue Time (30–40 minutes): Now it is time for your group members to dialogue about the things they are learning. Open up the dialogue with the following discussion questions. Some questions are new, from the fresh ideas I presented in the video segment. Others revisit some of the questions I asked in the daily workbook pages for this session, so that participants have a chance to talk over their workbook answers and gain insight from each other. If there are Scriptures connected to a particular question, encourage participation by asking a group member to read the Scripture aloud. Then read the discussion question to the group and ask for input.

Session 2 Discussion Questions

1. Day 1, question 1 in the workbook asked why even the merciful among us seem to find the mere thought of judging the wicked inspiring, and why even the merciful sometimes thirst to see others fall under judgment. What can we do individually and as prophetic communities to guard against that mindset?

2. In today's video, Kris referred to the prophecies of judgment that came forth against America after the 9-11 tragedy. How does that kind of prophecy go against our ministry as New Testament prophets and prophetesses, which is to release mercy on people who don't deserve it, because we don't deserve it either?

3. Day 2, question 4 asked you to name some ways in which negative prophetic voices have a negative impact on the lost rather than a positive impact. Besides the 9-11 example Kris gave in the book and video, have you seen other examples of that? What are some ways in which we can remind ourselves and each other to extend mercy rather than judgment?

4. After going through this video segment and session, what is your understanding of the difference between the roles of the New versus the Old Testament prophets and prophetesses?

Life Application Check (10 minutes): Now have participants answer the important question, "What do I do *next* to apply the principles I learned to my life and my spiritual walk?" Do this by going over the "Life Application" section from the workbook. Read it aloud and allow time for a couple testimonies of what group members did in response and what good things resulted from their efforts to apply this session to their lives.

If some participants have not done the applications for Sessions 1 and 2, urge them to go back and try them as soon as possible. Stress that making application is an important part of any study—possibly the most important part. Suggest that there is little point in studying spiritual principles at all if they have a net effect of zero on your life or ministry!

Closing Prayer/ Ministry (time will vary): Make any necessary announcements and mention that everyone should work through Session 3 in their workbook in preparation for next time. Offer a closing prayer to wrap up your meeting, or ask someone in the group to do so, and dismiss the group members to return home.

If time and space allow and there are those present who desire prayer or practice in prophetic ministry, invite them to stay. This ministry time may become a regular element at the close of your meetings. It can give the Holy Spirit room to move in people's lives in response to the lessons they have learned. It is also a good way to take the life application practice even further, providing a powerful conclusion to your meetings.

SESSION 3 GUIDE

Two Different Dispensations

In brief, Session 3 covers material from chapter 3 of *School of the Prophets*, along with the Session 3 pages from the participant workbook. In this session, I talk about two different dispensations: the *last days* (with an *s*) versus the *last day* (Judgment Day). Misunderstanding the dynamics of these two dispensations can lead to some seriously schizophrenic prophetic ministry. I show you from Scripture how the last days are days of mercy, favor and grace. These are the days we are in now. On the last day justice will be served, but it is not yet that day, and we are never the judge who hands down sentences and punishments. As prophets and prophetesses, we need to understand the times we live in, and we need to know how to minister in these times. I also relate in this session how I learned the hard way that prophecy and every other ministry in the Kingdom has to be rooted in love, which never fails.

Leadership Prayer Focus (before the meeting): Ask the Lord to help your participants identify the great and glorious days we are living in now, days of reconciliation and times in which we make every effort to find the gold in people. Ask that they would put on the mind of Christ when it comes to reconciliation versus judgment, and that they would know and understand how to minister prophetically in these times.

Welcome and Fellowship Time (20–30 minutes): Be ready 20 minutes before your meeting to start welcoming participants. Connect with each person as he or she arrives. Direct people to enjoy some fellowship (and refreshments if applicable) until the group begins. Check with any new participants about whether they have a *School of the Prophets* book and workbook, and help them get hold of the materials if needed. Ideally, participants will have worked through Session 3 by now, which is the material you will cover in this meeting.

Gather and Begin (10 minutes): Gather everyone together, along with their books, workbooks and something to write with. Introduce yourself and briefly outline the purpose of the group—to study *School of the Prophets* together and learn about developing a healthy prophetic community, along with gaining an understanding of the office of the prophet and prophetess in the Church today.

If you wish, allow participants to again give their names and perhaps one interesting fact about themselves, as they did at the first meeting. Briefly overview what the coming sessions will look like, and mention again that you will cover one session per meeting and that participants should read the materials and do the workbook pages for that session *prior* to the meetings. Encourage everyone to continue fully engaging with the curriculum to get the most out of this study.

Opening Prayer, Worship (10 minutes): Pray for the meeting aloud, or ask a group member to do so. If your group includes worship, enter into that now to prepare your hearts to receive whatever the Holy Spirit has for you in this meeting. Remember as group leader to put in place ahead of time your method for worship and double-check AV equipment so that it functions properly. Be alert in this time of worship since people may receive words of knowledge, wisdom or prophetic words.

Steward your participants' time well. Once you sense that the Holy Spirit is ready for you to move on into the study portion of your meeting, help the group make that transition. As before, gently direct those who might monopolize the group's time with personal problems to put their comments on hold and talk to you after the meeting. At that time, minister to them on a deeper level or direct them to an appropriate counselor in the church.

Video Teaching (20–30 minutes): At this point, transition into teaching time by having the group watch the video segment that goes along with Session 3. Participants should have workbooks and pens in hand so they can fill in the video guide in the workbook as they watch and listen. Again, make sure to test all AV equipment *prior* to your meeting.

Here are the answers for the Session 3 video guide. Review these answers with your group after the video so they can fill in any blanks they missed.

1. Your <u>job</u> (as a prophet or prophetess) is to find the <u>treasure</u> in the dirt of a person's life.
2. You don't have to be prophetic to find <u>sin</u> in sinners' lives, and you don't have to be prophetic to find <u>flaws</u> in the people you live with, but you have to be prophetic to find <u>goodness</u> in some people's lives.

3. God said, "Over My <u>dead</u> <u>body</u> will you go to hell," but there are people who <u>step</u> over His dead body and they <u>choose</u> hell.

4. God never <u>takes</u> <u>away</u> choice, because <u>love</u> requires <u>choice</u>.

5. There is a difference between the <u>last</u> <u>days</u> and the <u>last</u> <u>day</u>.

6. The last day is a day of <u>judgment</u>, and we are <u>never</u> the judge.

7. There is a day of judgment, but there are <u>last</u> <u>days</u> when God will pour His <u>Spirit</u> out on all <u>flesh.</u>

8. Those are <u>great</u> and <u>glorious</u> days, and everyone who calls on the name of the Lord in those days will be <u>saved</u>.

9. We live in the last days, NOT the last day, and so our ministry is still the ministry of <u>reconciliation</u>, and not <u>judgment</u>.

10. Between the <u>favorable</u> day of the Lord and the day of <u>vengeance</u> of our God (Judgment Day) are <u>thousands</u> of years.

11. A lot of people bring <u>Judgment</u> <u>Day</u> into the last days and end up with a very <u>schizophrenic</u> prophetic ministry.

Discussion/Dialogue Time (30–40 minutes): Now it is time for your group members to dialogue about the things they are learning. Open up the dialogue with the following discussion questions. If there are Scriptures connected to a particular question, encourage participation by asking a group member to read the Scripture aloud. Then read the discussion question to the group and ask for input.

Session 3 Discussion Questions ─────────────────

1. Kris said in today's video that when he was earnestly asking God for insight about offending people so much through his prophetic ministry, the Holy Spirit told him, "I'll convict people of sin; you convict them of the glory of God they fell short of." What does that mean to you in the sense of carrying out prophetic ministry?

2. From Day 1, question 3 in the workbook, why might "not counting people's trespasses against them" destroy the ministry of a few of the prophets and prophetesses of our time? Which dispensation are such judgmental prophets operating from? Which dispensation do they need to operate from?

3. We are supposed to be like Jesus and follow His example, yet Kris made the statement in this session that there are some things Jesus did that we should never do. What kind of things, and why not? How does that affect the way we minister prophetically?

4. From Day 4, question 4, why is it incumbent upon us as God's prophets and prophetesses to use our gifts to find the gold buried in the dirt of people's lives? What does that accomplish in people that finding and exposing all their sins would not?

Life Application Check (10 minutes): Now have participants answer the important question, "What do I do *next* to apply the principles I learned to my life and my spiritual walk?" Do this by going over the "Life Application" section from the workbook. Read it aloud and allow time for a couple testimonies of what group members did in response and what good things resulted from their efforts to apply this session to their lives.

If some participants have not done the applications for these early sessions, have them go back and try them. Stress again that application is an important part of any study—possibly the most important part.

Closing Prayer/Ministry (time will vary): Make any necessary announcements and mention that everyone should work through Session 4 in their workbook in preparation for next time. Offer a closing prayer to wrap up your meeting, or ask someone in the group to do so, and dismiss the group members to return home.

If time and space allow and there are those present who desire prayer or practice in prophetic ministry, invite them to stay. This ministry time can give the Holy Spirit room to move in people's lives in response to the lessons they have learned, and it can provide a powerful conclusion to your meetings.

SESSION 4 GUIDE

Prophetic Perspectives

In brief, Session 4 covers material from chapter 4 of *School of the Prophets*, along with the Session 4 pages from the participant workbook. I introduce the subject of core values in this session, which are the lenses through which we see life, live and minister. We will see how deeply our core values affect our behavior, and how, if they are damaged, scratched or faulty, they skew our perspective of God and reality. As prophets and prophetesses, we can skew others' perspectives through our ministry if we are acting out of faulty or damaged core values. (The Core Values Assessment Test in chapter 4 of the book will help each participant assess where he or she is at in terms of actual core values.) What we need is to assimilate healthy Kingdom core values, and in this session we will look at several of those values as they relate to prophetic ministry. Kingdom core values need to become the identity out of which we live and minister truth and freedom to others.

Leadership Prayer Focus (before the meeting): Ask the Lord to enlighten the eyes of your participants' hearts and to help them see through clear spiritual lenses. Ask Him to reveal to each one his or her actual core values and what is needed to adjust those values so that they come into line with Kingdom core values. Also ask Him to show your participants the importance of ministering out of healthy core values.

Welcome and Fellowship Time (20–30 minutes): Be ready 20 minutes before your meeting to start welcoming participants. Connect with each person as he or she arrives. Direct people to enjoy some fellowship (and refreshments if applicable) until the group begins. Check with any new participants about whether they have a *School of the Prophets* book and workbook, and help them get hold of the materials if needed. Ideally, participants will have worked through Session 4 by now, which is the material you will cover in this meeting.

Gather and Begin (10 minutes): Gather everyone together, along with their books, workbooks and something to write with. Introduce yourself and briefly outline the purpose of the group—to study *School of the Prophets* together and learn about developing a healthy prophetic community, along with gaining an understanding of the office of the prophet and prophetess in the Church today.

If you wish, allow participants to again give their names and perhaps one interesting fact about themselves. Briefly overview what the coming sessions will look like, and mention again that you will cover one session per meeting and that participants should read the materials and do the workbook pages for that session *prior* to the meetings. Encourage everyone to continue fully engaging with the curriculum to get the most out of this study.

Opening Prayer, Worship (10 minutes): Pray for the meeting aloud, or ask a group member to do so. If your group includes worship, enter into that now to prepare your hearts to receive whatever the Holy Spirit has for you in this meeting. Remember as group leader to put in place ahead of time your method for worship and double-check AV equipment so that it functions properly. Be alert in this time of worship since people may receive words of knowledge, wisdom or prophetic words.

Steward your participants' time well. Once you sense that the Holy Spirit is ready for you to move on into the study portion of your meeting, help the group make that transition. As before, gently direct those who might monopolize the group's time with personal problems to put their comments on hold and talk to you after the meeting. At that time, minister to them on a deeper level or direct them to an appropriate counselor in the church.

Video Teaching (20–30 minutes): At this point, transition into teaching time by having the group watch the video segment that goes along with Session 4. Participants should have workbooks and pens in hand so they can fill in the video guide in the workbook as they watch and listen. Again, make sure to test all AV equipment *prior* to your meeting.

Here are the answers for the Session 4 video guide. Review these answers with your group after the video so they can fill in any blanks they missed.

1. You see, hear and perceive the world with an <u>accent</u>.
2. You <u>view</u> the world not as it is, but as <u>you</u> are.
3. Core values are the <u>lenses</u> of your life . . . core values are the way you <u>see</u> life.
4. When a prophet says God is <u>angry</u>, it's pretty difficult not to have <u>judgmental</u> words.

5. The way I see God <u>affects</u> the way I do <u>ministry</u>.

6. If I believe God is loving, then I believe the <u>best</u> about people. I extend <u>mercy</u> to people; I look for <u>good</u> in people.

7. God is love, and <u>perfect</u> love casts out fear because fear involves <u>punishment</u>. Therefore, <u>prophetic</u> <u>words</u> should flow out of love, not out of fear.

8. When I prophesy and it creates fear and anxiety, I have <u>partnered</u> with the <u>wrong</u> spirit.

9. It takes the <u>Word</u> of God AND the <u>Spirit</u> of God to equal <u>reality</u> (truth).

10. When people <u>encounter</u> our prophetic gift, they should <u>encounter</u> God's <u>love</u>.

Discussion/Dialogue Time (30–40 minutes): Now it is time for your group members to dialogue about the things they are learning. Open up the dialogue with the following discussion questions. If there are Scriptures connected to a particular question, encourage participation by asking a group member to read the Scripture aloud. Then read the discussion question to the group and ask for input.

Session 4 Discussion Questions ―――――――――

1. In today's video, Kris made the comment that most people read the Bible to validate what they already believe, and that few people carry a spirit of revelation in which they come to the Bible ready to receive new revelation instead of using it to validate what they already believe. How can we make sure that we are approaching the Bible for revelation, not validation?

2. Kris focused in this session on developing and living out Kingdom core values. From Day 2, question 5, what were some of the ways you named in which having Kingdom core values manifests in a person's prophetic ministry?

3. Kingdom core values are the lenses through which we can see reality clearly and minister to others effectively. What was your response to your score on the Core Values Assessment Test that you took in the book during this session? What will you do to realign your core values with the Kingdom's core values where needed?

4. What do you think Kris meant when he suggested that having broken spiritual "lenses" is like having anorexia of the spirit, which perpetuates dysfunction, especially in prophetic ministry? What can we do to repair or replace damaged spiritual lenses?

Life Application Check (10 minutes): Now have participants answer the important question, "What do I do *next* to apply the principles I learned to my life and my spiritual walk?" Do this by going over the "Life Application" section from the workbook. Read it aloud and allow time for a couple testimonies of what group members did in response and what good things resulted from their efforts to apply this session to their lives.

In another of my books, *Spirit Wars* (Chosen, 2012), I include a section about how important it is to steward our testimonies. We put a high priority on doing that at Bethel Church, and we continue to see the fruits of it. This might be a good time to appoint someone in the group to write down the testimonies that come forth in your group conversations from this meeting onward. At each session, have that person come prepared to note down the testimonies in a special place. In your final meeting several sessions ahead, consider encouraging everyone by reading some of these testimonies back as part of your group wrap-up or conclusion celebration.

If some participants have not done the applications for these early sessions, have them go back and try them. Stress again that application is an important part of any study—possibly the most important part.

Closing Prayer/Ministry (time will vary): Make any necessary announcements and mention that everyone should work through Session 5 in their workbook in preparation for next time. Offer a closing prayer to wrap up your meeting, or ask someone in the group to do so, and dismiss the group members to return home.

If time and space allow and there are those present who desire prayer or practice in prophetic ministry, invite them to stay. This ministry time can give the Holy Spirit room to move in people's lives in response to the lessons they have learned, providing a powerful conclusion to your meetings.

SESSION 5 GUIDE
Prophecy versus Prophets

In brief, Session 5 covers material from chapter 5 of *School of the Prophets*, along with the Session 5 pages from the participant workbook. This session is all about the gift of prophecy versus the office of prophet or prophetess. Both are vital to the Body of Christ, but they are *not* the same thing. In the book I provide a gift-versus-office summary chart that should make the differences between them clear. Every believer can function in the gift, but some are also called by God to the office. I also spend a little time in this session talking about the difference between prophetic warnings and prophetic judgments, a difference that as prophetic people, we must grasp if we want to minister effectively this side of the cross to both the Church and to the lost.

Leadership Prayer Focus (before the meeting): Ask the Lord to clear up through this session any misunderstandings your participants may have regarding the difference between *having* the gift of prophecy and *being* the gift by holding a prophetic office. Ask that the Holy Spirit reveal to them the purpose of the gift (edification, exhortation and consolation) and the purpose of the office (to equip the saints to do the work of service in building up the Body).

Welcome and Fellowship Time (20–30 minutes): Be ready 20 minutes before your meeting to start welcoming participants. Connect with each person as he or she arrives. Direct people to enjoy some fellowship (and refreshments if applicable) until the group begins. Check with any new participants about whether they have a *School of the Prophets* book and workbook, and help them get hold of the materials if needed. Ideally, participants will have worked through Session 5 by now, which is the material you will cover in this meeting.

Gather and Begin (10 minutes): Gather everyone together, along with their books, workbooks and something to write with. Introduce yourself and briefly outline the purpose of the group—to study *School of the Prophets* together and learn about developing a healthy prophetic community, along with gaining an understanding of the office of the prophet and prophetess in the Church today.

If you wish, allow participants to again give their names and perhaps one interesting fact about themselves. Briefly overview what the remaining sessions will look like, and mention again that you will cover one session per meeting and that participants should read the materials and do the workbook pages for that session *prior* to the meetings. Encourage everyone to continue fully engaging with the curriculum to get the most out of this study.

Opening Prayer, Worship (10 minutes): Pray for the meeting aloud, or ask a group member to do so. If your group includes worship, enter into that now to prepare your hearts to receive whatever the Holy Spirit has for you in this meeting. Remember as group leader to put in place ahead of time your method for worship and double-check AV equipment. Be alert in this time of worship since people may receive words of knowledge, wisdom or prophetic words.

Steward your participants' time well. Once you sense that the Holy Spirit is ready for you to move on into the study portion of your meeting, help the group make that transition. As before, gently direct those who might monopolize the group's time with personal problems to put their comments on hold and talk to you after the meeting. At that time, minister to them on a deeper level or direct them to an appropriate counselor in the church.

Video Teaching (20–30 minutes): At this point, transition into teaching time by having the group watch the video segment that goes along with Session 5. Participants should have workbooks and pens in hand so they can fill in the video guide in the workbook as they watch and listen. Again, make sure to test all AV equipment *prior* to your meeting.

Here are the answers for the Session 5 video guide. Review these answers with your group after the video so they can fill in any blanks they missed.

1. You can't <u>earn</u> the <u>gift</u> of prophecy.
2. The gift of prophecy is a gift of the <u>Holy Spirit</u>; the office of the prophet is a gift of <u>Christ</u>.
3. No matter how many gifts the Holy Spirit has to give, we are taught to <u>especially</u> <u>desire</u> the gift of <u>prophecy</u>.
4. The gift of prophecy <u>builds</u> up, <u>cheers</u> up and <u>calls</u> people near.
5. The fruits of the Spirit are a sign that you are <u>maturing</u> in God; the gifts of the Spirit are a sign that you've received an <u>endowment</u> from God, which is a free <u>gift</u>.

6. God has called both <u>genders</u> to the <u>office</u> of prophet or prophetess.

7. If I am a prophet or prophetess, the gift is not <u>what</u> I <u>do</u>, it's <u>who</u> I <u>am</u>.

8. The <u>emphasis</u> of the office of a prophet is <u>equipping</u> the <u>saints</u>.

9. A prophet must be <u>anointed</u> by God AND have <u>people</u> to lead.

10. Often God calls us, and <u>later</u> people <u>recognize</u> the call.

11. We <u>acknowledge</u> prophets; we don't <u>create</u> them.

12. There's a huge difference between a <u>judgment</u> and a <u>warning</u>.

13. Don't do with <u>prophecy</u> what you should do with <u>discipleship</u> (fatherhood and motherhood).

Discussion/Dialogue Time (30–40 minutes): Now allow time for your group members to dialogue about the things they are learning. Open up the dialogue with the following discussion questions. If there are Scriptures connected to a particular question, encourage participation by asking a group member to read the Scripture aloud. Then read the discussion question to the group and ask for input.

Session 5 Discussion Questions _____

1. As Kris pointed out in both today's video and the book, there is a lot of confusion over the gift of prophecy and the office of prophet or prophetess. From Day 3, question 1 in the workbook, when it comes to the prophetic, what is the difference between *having* the gift and *being* the gift?

2. Since not everyone who prophesies holds the office of prophet or prophetess, from Day 3, question 5, at present which side of the gift-versus-office summary chart do you fall on? What differences between the two sides has the chart and this session clarified for you? How will this help you in your life and/or ministry?

3. How do you know whether you are moving in the gift of prophecy or you are called to the office of a prophet or prophetess? What are some indicators of being called to the office?

4. In this session, Kris strongly emphasized the difference between the prophetic warnings of our day and the Old Testament's prophetic judgments. From Day 4, question 3, how are the two different? Why is it incorrect to call warnings judgments?

Life Application Check (10 minutes): Now have participants answer the important question, "What do I do *next* to apply the principles I learned to my life and my spiritual walk?" Do this by going over the "Life Application" section from the workbook. Read it aloud and allow time for a couple testimonies of what group members did in response and what good things resulted from their efforts to apply this session to their lives.

If some participants have not done the applications for any sessions, have them go back and try them. Stress again that application is an important part of any study—possibly the most important part.

*Closing Prayer/Ministry (**time will vary**):* Make any necessary announcements and mention that everyone should work through Session 6 in their workbook in preparation for next time. Offer a closing prayer to wrap up your meeting, or ask someone in the group to do so, and dismiss the group members to return home.

If time and space allow and there are those present who desire prayer or practice in prophetic ministry, invite them to stay. This ministry time can give the Holy Spirit room to move in people's lives in response to the lessons they have learned, providing a powerful conclusion to your meetings.

SESSION 6 GUIDE
The Role of the Prophet

In brief, Session 6 covers material from chapter 6 of *School of the Prophets*, along with the Session 6 pages from the participant workbook. I start this session by looking at Ezra prophesying over the valley of dry bones, and I explore with you the implications that has for us in speaking life into death with our prophetic words. Prophets build worlds with words; it is one of their primary roles. Prophets also have the role of equipping the saints for the work of service, to build up the Body. My soda fountain illustration of the fivefold ministers, although somewhat unusual, provides deeper insight into how that works. Some other prophetic roles I talk about in this session are equipping others to hear from God, providing prophetic role models, commissioning leaders in various arenas (including secular governments), acting as God's Secret Service and protecting the nations while simultaneously extending the ministry of reconciliation to unbelievers (no small balancing act). With all these roles to fill, there is no shortage of ministry opportunities for prophets and prophetesses.

Leadership Prayer Focus (before the meeting): Ask the Lord to give each participant, particularly those called to the office of a prophet or prophetess, insight into the many roles those with the office play in bringing the Kingdom of heaven to earth. Ask that your participants' eyes and ears be opened to the wonder of building worlds with words and speaking life into death through powerful and effective prophetic ministry.

Welcome and Fellowship Time (20–30 minutes): Be ready 20 minutes before your meeting to start welcoming participants. Connect with each person as he or she arrives. Direct people to enjoy some fellowship (and refreshments if applicable) until the group begins. Check with any new participants about whether they have a *School of the Prophets* book and workbook, and help them get hold of the materials if needed. Ideally, participants will have worked through Session 6 by now, which is the material you will cover in this meeting.

Gather and Begin (10 minutes): Gather everyone together, along with their books, workbooks and something to write with. Introduce yourself and briefly outline the purpose of the group—to study *School of the Prophets* together and learn about developing a healthy prophetic community, along with gaining an understanding of the office of the prophet and prophetess in the Church today.

If you wish, allow participants to again give their names and perhaps one interesting fact about themselves. Briefly overview what the remaining sessions will look like, and mention again that you will cover one session per meeting and that participants should read the materials and do the workbook pages for that session *prior* to the meetings. Encourage everyone to continue fully engaging with the curriculum to get the most out of this study.

Opening Prayer, Worship (10 minutes): Pray for the meeting aloud, or ask a group member to do so. If your group includes worship, enter into that now to prepare your hearts to receive whatever the Holy Spirit has for you in this meeting. Remember as group leader to put in place ahead of time your method for worship and double-check AV equipment. Be alert in this time of worship since people may receive words of knowledge, wisdom or prophetic words.

Steward your participants' time well. Once you sense that the Holy Spirit is ready for you to move on into the study portion of your meeting, help the group make that transition. As before, gently direct those who might monopolize the group's time with personal problems to put their comments on hold and talk to you after the meeting. At that time, minister to them on a deeper level or direct them to an appropriate counselor in the church.

Video Teaching (20–30 minutes): At this point, transition into teaching time by having the group watch the video segment that goes along with Session 6. Participants should have workbooks and pens in hand so they can fill in the video guide in the workbook as they watch and listen. Again, make sure to test all AV equipment *prior* to your meeting.

Here are the answers for the Session 6 video guide. Review these answers with your group after the video so they can fill in any blanks they missed.

1. Words become <u>worlds</u>. We're not on the eve of <u>destruction</u>; we're on the eve of <u>construction</u>.
2. <u>Prophets</u> change history. Sometimes they change history on their <u>knees</u> in prophetic prayer, and sometimes they change history when they prophesy the <u>direction</u> to kings.

3. Romans 12:6 says, "Since we have gifts that differ according to the <u>grace</u> given to us, each of us is to <u>exercise</u> them accordingly: if prophecy, according to the proportion of his <u>faith</u> . . ."

4. Grace is the <u>operational</u> <u>power</u> of God that gives me the ability to do what I couldn't do one <u>second</u> before I received the grace.

5. The <u>primary</u> job of the <u>pastor</u> is to equip the saints with pastoral grace so that the <u>saints</u> can take care of the saints.

6. The goal of the <u>prophet</u> is that you would have eyes to see and ears to hear so that the <u>Body</u> can take care of the <u>need</u> that the Body has for prophetic revelation and prophetic ministry to comfort, build up and console.

7. Prophets <u>commission</u> leaders.

8. Oftentimes God calls <u>prophets</u> to <u>commission</u> kings and governors and mayors.

9. If we (as prophets) <u>withdraw</u> from people who don't know God, there will be no <u>light</u> in their life.

10. We create <u>atmospheres</u> of prophetic <u>presence</u> where people can have experiences with God and become who they were meant to be.

Discussion/Dialogue Time (30–40 minutes): Now allow time for your group members to dialogue about the things they are learning. Open up the dialogue with the following discussion questions. If there are Scriptures connected to a particular question, encourage participation by asking a group member to read the Scripture aloud. Then read the discussion question to the group and ask for input.

Session 6 Discussion Questions _____

1. In Kris's book and video illustration of a soda fountain representing the fivefold ministers (apostles, prophets, evangelists, pastors and teachers), all five flavors at the fountain had one thing in common: soda water. What does the soda water represent in the spiritual? Believers come to the fountain to receive grace from each of the fivefold ministers in order to do what?

2. What do you think Kris meant by his statement in today's video that "prophets and prophetesses are the ones who are responsible as equippers to hook up the telephone in the temple—in each temple—that's our job"?

3. From Day 2, question 4 in the workbook, what does it signify about a spiritual community when its prophets and prophetesses become everyone's main source of hearing from God? What are some of the results of that scenario?

4. In what way is Kris as the senior prophet of the Bethel movement just the equipment guy who is handing out equipment to the saints?

Life Application Check (10 minutes): Now have participants answer the important question, "What do I do *next* to apply the principles I learned to my life and my spiritual walk?" Do this by going over the "Life Application" section from the workbook. Read it aloud and allow time for a couple testimonies of what group members did in response and what good things resulted from their efforts to apply this session to their lives.

If some participants have not done the applications for any sessions, have them go back and try them. Stress again that application is an important part of any study—possibly the most important part.

Closing Prayer/Ministry (time will vary): Make any necessary announcements and mention that everyone should work through Session 7 in their workbook in preparation for next time. Offer a closing prayer to wrap up your meeting, or ask someone in the group to do so, and dismiss the group members to return home.

If time and space allow and there are those present who desire prayer or practice in prophetic ministry, invite them to stay. This ministry time can give the Holy Spirit room to move in people's lives in response to the lessons they have learned, providing a powerful conclusion to your meetings.

Session 7 Guide
Building a Prophetic Community

In brief, Session 7 covers material from chapter 7 of *School of the Prophets*, along with the Session 7 pages from the participant workbook. In this session, I explore the things leaders can do to develop a healthy prophetic culture—things like coaching and giving feedback, confronting in a positive way, being in charge but not being controlling, and providing safety but also the opportunity for people to take risks in order to grow. I highlight the need to establish an R&D (research and development) culture versus a zero defects culture when it comes to training for the prophetic. (Certainly, there is a place where we should strive for zero defects spiritually, and I talk more about that in the pages of the book. But the area of prophetic growth is not that place.) Finally, I look at some of the practical necessities of leading a prophetic community, things like being able to de-escalate anger, dispel gossip, encourage testimonies, shepherd superheroes and help people face their fears, all so your prophetic people can minister more effectively.

Leadership Prayer Focus (before the meeting): Ask the Lord to give your participants a heart to develop fathers and mothers, coaches and referees within their prophetic communities so that feedback, positive confrontation and a great deal of encouragement can take place. Ask that rather than being wary of risk, they begin to foster a culture of risk-taking to promote growth. Finally, pray that they train prophetic people with their deployment in mind beyond home base, paying attention to protocol where previously it may have been downplayed or overlooked.

Welcome and Fellowship Time (20–30 minutes): Be ready 20 minutes before your meeting to start welcoming participants. Connect with each person as he or she arrives. Direct people to enjoy some fellowship (and refreshments if applicable) until the group begins. Check with any new participants about whether they have a *School of the Prophets* book and workbook, and help them get hold of the materials if needed. (Since you are nearing the conclusion of your study, suggest that any newcomers sign up for an upcoming *School of the Prophets* group, if one will be available. If not, they can still benefit from going back and studying the book and workbook individually.) Ideally, participants will have worked through Session 7 by now, which is the material you will cover in this meeting.

Gather and Begin (10 minutes): Gather everyone together, along with their books, workbooks and something to write with. Introduce yourself and briefly outline the purpose of the group—to study *School of the Prophets* together and learn about developing a healthy prophetic community, along with gaining an understanding of the office of the prophet and prophetess in the Church today.

If you wish, allow participants to again give their names and perhaps one interesting fact about themselves. Briefly overview what the remaining sessions will look like, and mention again that you will cover one session per meeting and that participants should read the materials and do the workbook pages for that session *prior* to the meetings. Encourage everyone to continue fully engaging with the curriculum to get the most out of this study.

Opening Prayer, Worship (10 minutes): Pray for the meeting aloud, or ask a group member to do so. If your group includes worship, enter into that now to prepare your hearts to receive whatever the Holy Spirit has for you in this meeting. Remember as group leader to put in place ahead of time your method for worship and double-check AV equipment. Be alert in this time of worship since people may receive words of knowledge, wisdom or prophetic words.

Steward your participants' time well. Once you sense that the Holy Spirit is ready for you to move on into the study portion of your meeting, help the group make that transition. As before, gently direct those who might monopolize the group's time with personal problems to put their comments on hold and talk to you after the meeting. At that time, minister to them on a deeper level or direct them to an appropriate counselor in the church.

Video Teaching (20–30 minutes): At this point, transition into teaching time by having the group watch the video segment that goes along with Session 7. Participants should have workbooks and pens in hand so they can fill in the video guide in the workbook as they watch and listen. Again, make sure to test all AV equipment *prior* to your meeting.

Here are the answers for the Session 7 video guide. Review these answers with your group after the video so they can fill in any blanks they missed.

1. There's a difference between prophetic <u>ministry</u> and a prophetic <u>community</u>.

2. There are <u>fathers</u> and <u>mothers</u>, <u>coaches</u> and <u>referees</u>, metaphorically speaking, who help us learn the "game" of prophecy.

3. It's not practice that makes perfect, it's <u>perfect</u> <u>practice</u> that makes perfect. If you practice something the <u>wrong</u> way long enough, it becomes a <u>habit</u> and it's difficult to change.

4. It's okay for leadership to <u>critique</u> how we're doing (in prophetic ministry). <u>Feedback</u> is the way we grow.

5. Part of growing a prophetic community is that to the level that you <u>empower</u> people, you <u>confront</u> them.

6. We don't want to develop a culture of <u>punishment</u>, because as soon as we do that, we take away the culture where we're confronting in a <u>redemptive</u> way.

7. We have to <u>train</u> and <u>equip</u> with <u>deployment</u> in mind.

8. You may be determining your <u>metron</u>, your sphere of influence, by your <u>manifestation</u>.

9. It doesn't hurt to keep <u>protocol</u>; it's not the fear of man. You give <u>honor</u> to whom <u>honor</u> is due.

10. God likes <u>order</u>. Paul said let <u>all</u> <u>things</u> be done decently and in order.

11. As prophets and prophetesses, it's our job to help <u>coach</u> and ref our people so that we actually begin to help create a prophetic <u>community</u> and a prophetic <u>culture</u>.

12. A prophetic culture is a culture of <u>safety</u>, but it's also a culture of <u>risk</u>.

Discussion/Dialogue Time (30–40 minutes): Now allow time for your group members to dialogue about the things they are learning. Open up the dialogue with the following discussion questions. If there are Scriptures connected to a particular question, encourage participation by asking a group member to read the Scripture aloud. Then read the discussion question to the group and ask for input.

Session 7 Discussion Questions ⸺⸺⸺⸺⸺⸺⸺

1. Feedback is how we grow. Kris said in today's video that the goal is to have prophetic communities where people are expecting that there will be fathers and mothers speaking to them about how they are doing. Is feedback currently part of your prophetic community (or your church that needs to establish a healthy prophetic community)? What could be done to take this important element to a new level, while keeping it positive?

2. Speaking of feedback, what did Kris mean by saying that if you empower people without confronting them, you will end up with Absaloms?

3. In the video, Kris asked what seems like an amusing question, but is actually an important one: Are you helping yourself by being "weird" in your prophetic ministry? If you are training with deployment anywhere outside your own culture in mind (standing before kings, for example, or at the mall in front of the lost), how does that affect your answer to that question?

4. A prophetic culture is a culture of safety, but it is also a culture of risk. From Day 1, question 3 in the workbook, in what way can prophetic ministry grow best in an R&D (research and development) culture? Why does a "zero defect" core value shut down that growth?

Life Application Check (10 minutes): Now have participants answer the important question, "What do I do *next* to apply the principles I learned to my life and my spiritual walk?" Do this by going over the "Life Application" section from the workbook. Read it aloud and allow time for a couple testimonies of what group members did in response and what good things resulted from their efforts to apply this session to their lives.

If some participants have not done the applications for any sessions, have them go back and try them. Stress again that application is an important part of any study—possibly the most important part.

Closing Prayer/Ministry (time will vary): Make any necessary announcements and mention that everyone should work through Session 8 in their workbook in preparation for next time. Remind everyone that Session 8 is the last meeting that will cover specific curriculum pages. If you are holding an optional ninth session to do a wrap-up or a fellowship outing, let your participants know (or decide) what that final meeting will involve. Offer a closing prayer to wrap up your meeting, or ask someone in the group to do so, and dismiss the group members to return home.

If time and space allow and there are those present who desire prayer or practice in prophetic ministry, invite them to stay. This ministry time can give the Holy Spirit room to move in people's lives in response to the lessons they have learned, providing a powerful conclusion to your meetings.

SESSION 8 GUIDE
Standing before Kings; Noble Prophets

In brief, Session 8 covers material from chapters 8 and 9 of *School of the Prophets*, along with the Session 8 pages from the participant workbook. In this session, I define what it means to be a prophet *to the nations* or a prophet and/or father *of the nations*. We draw wisdom from the lives of the prophets Joseph and Daniel, and we look at how they became an influential part of the foreign cultures they lived in without compromising their character. Their ministry to and love for foreign kings gives us much insight into how we can relate effectively to the high-level leaders of our time and powerfully minister to them. I also talk about several other prophetic models besides Joseph and Daniel, and about honoring each other in our prophetic diversity.

Leadership Prayer Focus (before the meeting): Ask the Lord to give your participants the courage to speak to kings and leaders if that is their call, and to extend encouragement to people of influence (rather than passing judgment), keeping in mind that it is the goodness of God that draws people to repentance. Ask that they come to value the wide diversity among prophets and prophetesses and to honor those with different prophetic DNA than they have, realizing that it takes all kinds of prophets to make the world go round.

Welcome and Fellowship Time (20–30 minutes): Be ready 20 minutes before your meeting to start welcoming participants. Connect with each person as he or she arrives. Direct people to enjoy some fellowship (and refreshments if applicable) until the group begins. Check with any new participants about whether they have a *School of the Prophets* book and workbook, and help them get hold of the materials if needed. (Since you are at the conclusion of your study, suggest that any newcomers sign up for an upcoming *School of the Prophets* group, if one will be available. If not, they can still benefit from going back and studying the book and workbook individually.) Ideally, participants will have worked through Session 8 by now, which is the material you will cover in this meeting.

Gather and Begin (10 minutes): Gather everyone together, along with their books, workbooks and something to write with. Introduce yourself and briefly outline the purpose of the group—to study *School of the Prophets* together and learn about developing a healthy prophetic community, along with gaining an understanding of the office of the prophet and prophetess in the Church today.

If you wish, allow participants to give their names and perhaps one interesting fact about themselves one more time. If you are holding an optional ninth session, briefly overview what that will involve. It may be a wrap-up meeting with more dialogue about points throughout this study that you all wish to return to, or perhaps it will be some kind of fellowship party or meal together to celebrate all you have learned and all the Lord has done through this study. Perhaps it will be a time for people in the group to practice the prophetic based on the principles they have learned. (Your participants should now be done with the *School of the Prophets* book and workbook.)

Opening Prayer, Worship (10 minutes): Pray for the meeting aloud, or ask a group member to do so. If your group includes worship, enter into that now to prepare your hearts to receive whatever the Holy Spirit has for you in this meeting. Remember as group leader to put in place ahead of time your method for worship and double-check AV equipment. Be alert in this time of worship since people may receive words of knowledge, wisdom or prophetic words.

Steward your participants' time well. Once you sense that the Holy Spirit is ready for you to move on into the study portion of your meeting, help the group make that transition. As before, gently direct those who might monopolize the group's time with personal problems to put their comments on hold and talk to you after the meeting. At that time, minister to them on a deeper level or direct them to an appropriate counselor in the church.

Video Teaching (20–30 minutes): At this point, transition into teaching time by having the group watch the video segment that goes along with Session 8. Participants should have workbooks and pens in hand so they can fill in the video guide in the workbook as they watch and listen. Again, make sure to test all AV equipment *prior* to your meeting.

Here are the answers for the Session 8 video guide. Review these answers with your group after the video so they can fill in any blanks they missed.

1. A prophet to nations speaks *to* them about <u>what</u> they should do. A prophet of a nation becomes a <u>part</u> of that nation and a <u>father</u> of that nation.
2. You are inherently nobility because your daddy is God.
3. Nobility in the Kingdom is that we get to bring out the best in people.

4. We need people who are full of <u>life</u>, <u>light</u> and <u>wisdom</u> to be interacting with and to be influencers of and leaders of nations.

5. God has a <u>purpose</u> for your life and <u>50 plans</u> to get you there.

6. Between the promise and the palace is a <u>process</u>, and that process is what <u>refines</u> your <u>character</u> so you can stay in the palace.

7. Small <u>keys</u> open huge <u>doors</u>.

8. Daniel is part of the <u>culture</u> without <u>compromising</u> his character.

9. It's hard for us to <u>judge</u> from the outside what somebody's <u>heart</u> is like on the inside.

10. The higher people get, the more <u>isolated</u> they are, and the more <u>encouragement</u> they need.

11. It's Jesus who is <u>water</u> to people's souls, flowing <u>through</u> us—water to their souls and <u>anointing</u> on their destinies.

Discussion/Dialogue Time (30–40 minutes): Now allow time for your group members to dialogue about the things they are learning. Open up the dialogue with the following discussion questions. If there are Scriptures connected to a particular question, encourage participation by asking a group member to read the Scripture aloud. Then read the discussion question to the group and ask for input.

Session 8 Discussion Questions

1. Kris asked in today's video, if as prophets and prophetesses we're not discipling the nations, who is? He also asked, if *somebody* is leading the nations and we don't think we have what it takes spiritually to be involved, what is happening in the vacuum of our low self-esteem? How would you answer those questions? In what sense is our false humility killing the nations?

2. Joseph and Daniel were both prophets who had a major impact on Gentile kings and nations. Through this session, what most stood out to you about their approach that made them so influential and effective in a foreign culture? How did their approach show that love never fails? What ramifications does that have for our prophetic ministry to the world and the political leaders of our day?

3. Kris talked a lot in this session about being a prophet *to* or *of* the nations. From Day 1, question 3 in the workbook, what is the difference between being a prophet *to the nations* and being a prophet *of the nations*?

4. Have you had the sense, as Kris has, that there is something going on in the spiritual between the decrees of kings and the proclamations of prophets, and that God is calling civil leaders and the fivefold ministry to walk together and help one another create synergy for good? What are some indications you have seen of that?

Life Application Check (10 minutes): Now have participants answer the important question, "What do I do *next* to apply the principles I learned to my life and my spiritual walk?" Do this by going over the "Life Application" section from the workbook. Read it aloud and allow time for a couple testimonies of what group members did in response and what good things resulted from their efforts to apply this session to their lives.

If some participants have not done the applications for any of the previous sessions, have them commit to going back and trying them. Stress one final time that application is an important part of any study—possibly the most important part.

Closing Prayer/Ministry (time will vary): Make any necessary announcements and mention that everyone should now be finished with the *School of the Prophets* book and workbook. Remind everyone that this was the last meeting that covered specific book and workbook pages, but that they can go back on their own and finish any sessions or readings they missed before they conclude their personal study of this curriculum.

If this is your final meeting and time allows, this conclusion time might be a good opportunity to ask for testimonies of what God has done in the participants' lives and ministry through this study. I have mentioned how important it is to steward the testimonies, and I am sure that the stories that come forth will amaze and encourage the group. If you appointed someone back in Session 4 to steward your group's testimonies by writing them down, now would be a good time to encourage everyone by reading those testimonies back to the group. (Or include that activity as part of your wrap-up or conclusion celebration if you are having a ninth session.)

Offer a closing prayer to wrap up your meeting, or ask someone in the group to do so, and dismiss the group members to return home. If there are still those present who desire prayer or practice in prophetic ministry, invite them to stay. Make sure as leader that even though your group meetings are at an end, anyone who needs additional counsel has been connected with someone in your group or church who can move them forward in their understanding of the role of both the gift of prophecy and the office of prophet and prophetess in today's Church.

If you are holding an optional ninth session to do a wrap-up or fellowship outing, let your participants know what that final meeting will involve for next time. Make sure everyone knows where and when that meeting will take place, if different from your usual meeting site, day or time. You may want to invite your participants to come ready with their testimonies of what God has done through this study, so that you can celebrate their testimonies at that final meeting. (If your group has been keeping a written record of the testimonies, you can use it at that meeting to encourage everyone.)

OPTIONAL FINAL MEETING
Practicing the Prophetic

This final session is optional. Your group participants should all be finished with the *School of the Prophets* curriculum. In the first eight sessions the book has been read, the workbook has been filled out, the videos have been viewed and the questions have been discussed, so you do not have any curriculum to cover at this meeting. Yet perhaps your group is not ready to disband or move on without some sort of wrap-up to the time you have spent together, learning about how to develop in prophetic ministry both personally and on a community level. If you feel your group would benefit from a final session to finish processing the materials, or if your participants want to come back to some points and finish discussing them in more depth, this would be an ideal time to set aside for that kind of wrap-up.

To make this ninth and final session memorable, you could choose from several options. Perhaps you will want to share a meal together for this conclusion meeting, along with sharing some testimonies of what the Holy Spirit has accomplished in your lives through *School of the Prophets*. Your group could meet at a local restaurant as a special activity, or you could hold a dinner at someone's home. There may even be a few culinary artists among you who would love to prepare a celebratory meal for the group. Or you could arrange a potluck where everyone contributes to the meal.

Another option would be to have a prophetic practice session together, based on the principles you have learned in this study. Practicing is a great way to get over any fears you may have and get feedback. Here is a prophetic exercise you could try similar to the example I told you about in the book, where I had new students at Bethel School of Supernatural Ministry practice with each other in the first week: Pray and ask the Lord for a word of knowledge for someone in your group. Be open to however He might respond to this prayer. Then pray quietly as you listen. You might feel a sensation in your body that indicates where someone is in need of healing. You might get an impression of a name or a picture. If you are working with a partner, ask if this has a particular meaning. If you are working in a group, tell your group leader, who can then bring it to the group. Try to be as specific as possible. Remember to always discern where any information is coming from. Also remember that the point of these exercises is not to "get it right" every time. The point is to celebrate practicing and risk-taking as a way to grow in the prophetic.

Whatever method you choose to wrap up your *School of the Prophets* study, make it a meaningful celebration of your time together. Your group has come a long way, covering a lot of scriptural and spiritual territory in new depth as you learned more about the gift of prophecy and the office itself. You have also studied many of the best ways to lead in developing a healthy prophetic community, and this final session would be an excellent time to put some of those principles into practice. If your group is part of the same prophetic community, do some analysis together of your prophetic culture's strengths and of some areas you could strengthen by making adjustments based on what you have learned through *School of the Prophets*.

As you conclude your final session, let the words of Jesus, spoken from the Messiah's chair, encourage you as you follow Him and answer His call in your prophetic ministry:

> The Spirit of the Lord is upon Me,
> Because He anointed Me to preach the gospel to the poor.
> He has sent Me to proclaim release to the captives,
> And recovery of sight to the blind,
> To set free those who are oppressed,
> To proclaim the favorable year of the Lord.
>
> Luke 4:18–19

Kris Vallotton has been happily married to his wife, Kathy, since 1975. They have four children and eight grandchildren. Three of their children are in full-time vocational ministry. Kris is the co-founder and senior overseer of the Bethel School of Supernatural Ministry, which has grown to more than two thousand full-time students. He is also the founder and president of Moral Revolution, an organization dedicated to cultural transformation.

Kris is the senior associate leader of Bethel Church in Redding, California, and has served with Bill Johnson since 1978. He has written and co-authored numerous books, and his revelatory insight and humorous delivery make him a much-sought-after international conference speaker.

You can contact Kris or find out more about him and his other ministry materials at www.kvministries.com, or you can download the KV Ministries app on your smartphone. You can also follow Kris and Kathy on their Facebook fan page at www.facebook.com/kvministries.